is the American...

knew that he had never...to fou...

...re who says he has no money 'really'...a deci-

As we shall see in Chapte...

...ist in a loss of the sense of the realness o...

...facts that can be consensually va...presses the 'existe...

...with his wife...

...t would have been psychotic, for instance, if, instead

...that the woman with whom he had intercourse was

...true because in this existential sense his 'real' wife

...ct of his own imagination (a phantom or image)

...the other human being in bed...

...bodied self of the schizoid individual cannot really be

anyone. It exists in perpetual isolation. And yet, ...

...isolation and inner non-commitment are not without

...on.

...thing final and definitive...

...cluding final and definitive about an act, which this

...n regards with suspicion. Action is the dead end of...

...ct must be of such an equivocal nature that the self...

...trapped in it.

...9, pp. 349–50) says this about the act:

something simple...

41
1000

Graham Stuart

# SHREDDED
# &
# PULPED

GRAHAM STEWART

..To my mother and father

PUBLISHED IN 2000
BY NSAD PRESS

EDITION 1000
ISBN 1 872482 36 8

---

DESIGN: ALI MUSA
FONT: ADOBE GARAMOND

# CONTENTS

# PREFACE

GRAHAM STEWART

Books are first and foremost convenient vehicles of
knowledge; and reflect the depth and extreme diversity
of human society, they are also symbols of achievement
and have over time become objects of status. Walk
through the doors of any library, and one is immediately
aware of a particular system for laying out the books in
a rational display of knowledge; an open, comprehensive
means to make available all of recorded human
experience to the visitor. When browsing at random
through any of the listed subjects I am continually
reminded of the competing, often conflicting critical
positions of so many acknowledged experts. Their
writings and hypotheses are part of a continuing battle
of ideas, and to me this struggle represents a potent
image of contemporary life. Equally apparent is that my
own scant knowledge of the vast majority of the
subjects so neatly shelved and stacked, is in all
probability inadequate to either contest or contribute to
the development of most of the arguments being so
eloquently expressed. Evidently I am, like so many
others, outside those debates. Of course it is much
easier if one has set aside some time and studied a
chosen subject in depth; that is perhaps an obvious
even disingenuous position, however it seems that ours
is an increasingly sectarian culture, and to accrue
substantial useful knowledge beyond our own

immediate interest is now next to impossible.

Simply coming to terms with one's own language deployed in unfamiliar conjunctions, where only the occasional paragraph or sentence seems sensible, merely emphasises the difficulty of gaining a tangible overall grasp of what may really be happening 'out there.' In the wake of these rapidly expanding fronts a strange pleasure emerges attendant, with reading a page of obscure fractured English, a form of aesthetic relish where clearly unable to follow the intended discourse, *but not to be denied*, one assumes the role of a detective, scratching around for clues, extracting parallel connections, or like Dr. Frankenstein, cutting and pasting unlikely combinations together ad hoc. This suggests both an intuitive 'DIY' reading, and an analytical forensic means of comprehension. In this way a randomly dismembered and reconstituted page can become a field of continuous open interpretation, more akin to certain types of live poetry or painting.

Having heard of R D. Laings' work and something of his reputation as a modern renaissance man, I began to consider which of his writings would most suit my purposes. I obtained my first copy of his seminal introduction to existential psychoanalysis *The Divided Self* in Seattle some six years ago. It happened to be a first edition in good condition, and I was pleased to have such a handsome example to read from.

Contained in this, my first publication, are reproductions of the eleven shredded, mulched and pressed chapters of *The Divided Self*, along with the Preface, Acknowledgments, References, and Index. The contents of each is re-presented here on two sides, the front and reverse of each page. Accompanying the progress of the shredded sections are two essays; one entitled "The Gutenberg Fetish", by the author and poet George Szirtes, and the other "Reading Material", by the artist Buzz Spector. There is also an introduction by Dr. Leon Redler and a photo essay by Yukimozo, entitled "Some Of My Best Friends Are Stones".

I have been working both as Yukimozo and as Graham Stewart since 1992. Dividing my practice in this way has allowed me to generate discrete individual identities and activities for both parties, and sufficient space to develop otherwise irrational schemes into concrete projects. This book is in effect a book of a shredded book and takes the whole recycled, reified book project, begun in 1991, one full revolution. Being in part about the tension between creation and destruction, and the problems arising from defining sanity and madness, it provides an ideal vehicle for them to work together for the first time. ■

## ACKNOWLEDGEMENTS

Thanks are due to the Norwich School of Art & Design Research Committee for their generous financial support of this project, to George Szirtes and Buzz Spector for their thoughtful essays, and to Dr. Redler for his perceptive introduction. Special thanks also to Ali Musa whose good judgment and sound sense of design was pivotal in bringing this project to a successful conclusion, and to Ben Taylor at NSAD for his invaluable advice on all matters photographic. And finally, to Bruce Desjardines, who has for a number of years collected my work and has contributed substantially to the funding of this book.

The dissecting room and the slaughterhouse furnished many of my materials; and often did my human nature turn with loathing from my occupation, whilst, still urged on by an eagerness which perpetually increased, I brought my work near to a conclusion. ■ Mary Shelley, *Frankenstein*.

# INTRODUCTION

DR. LEON REDLER

In the uncertainty and confusion following the fall of the Shah, Americans quickly began shredding documents deemed to be 'sensitive' at their soon to be occupied embassy. Young Iranian students and Revolutionary Guards worked patiently and persistently for two years to reconstitute these documents from the shredded bits of paper.

Graham Stewart, who referred to their work when telling me of his own, maintains that Humpty Dumpty could always have been put together again if only 'all the King's Horses and all the King's Men' had the patience, fervour and, perhaps, the technology of those young Iranians.

One day, millennia from now, some of our descendants may find Graham's transformation of a copy of *The Divided Self*, by R.D. Laing, one of the seminal books of our time. Who knows what they may make of this new found object, found under who knows what circumstances? Will they think and care to reverse Graham's process and "read thoroughly" the reconstituted book?

I hardly know what to make of it now. The creator of this shredded book object is moved by faces in stones and the silent testimony of selected shredded and reconstituted books. He is a finder of stones that face and speak to him, facing us with them. Taking the mass

produced book as a material object, he has created one
that, as object, calls for our attention. He goes beyond
and is doing something other than defacing the book,
he argues, as he keeps it potentially intact (for those
sufficiently motivated and resourced).

Here, he begins with a book on 'sanity' and 'madness,'
one that addresses how we are, or may become, divided
(hidden, disembodied, broken hearted and with 'a false
self system' operating in the world ), how our way of
being and our way of relating to others can become
shredded, manipulating and manipulated. He proceeds
to shred, mash, paste and in other ways manipulate the
matter at hand into a new artefact, a new facet or fact
of his art. There's more than a trace of iconoclast in
him yet he's created an icon which will appeal to
selected collectors.

He approached me to write an introduction to this
special, limited edition as I worked with Ronnie Laing
and continue to be instructed and inspired by what he
taught me. Laing's work is currently being seriously
reassessed, ten years after his death, with a proliferation
of books and conferences on his life and work,
particularly in the USA and the UK. But the psychiatric
profession has yet to open itself to the provocation and
challenge of Laing's intelligent and passionate critique.
Most psychiatrists have not yet taken *The Divided Self*

on board, and certainly not to heart... which is more to the point!

Perhaps the questioning and controversy that Graham Stewart's work will engender will lead some to read, or reread, the undivided and unshredded text to see whether Laing's existential-phenomenological accounts of the 'schizoid' condition and of madness may or may not shed any light on our own condition, as well as on Graham's iconoclastic icon-making at the end of this century and millennium, at a time when "the end of the subject" and "the end of the book" are increasingly spoken of but, as yet, insufficiently understood as to their profound implications.

May this book, and what it may provoke, be enjoyed by its holders and beholders, in their own way and in their own time. ■

# TO MAKE A SHREDDED BOOK

## INGREDIENTS

One book

One shredding machine

One sharp knife

Several plastic bags

A kettle

A metal bucket

Two Formica boards (9mm)

Four medium clamps

A spatula

A wire mesh baking tray

1. Take one whole publication and read thoroughly. Using a sharp knife remove the casing and keep to one side. Divide the remainder into preferred sections or keep as one large section.

2. Pass each section sideways, one or two pages at a time, through your chosen shredding machine. Carefully collect all the strips of fractured text into appropriately labelled bags. Do this for each section until the book is completely dismembered.

3. Empty the contents of one bag into a large metal bucket and pour several pints of boiling water over the paper strips. Leave to soak for a few minutes, stir once or twice, and drain thoroughly.

4. Gather the wet paper mulch and set it out onto a non-absorbent flat surface (Formica boards are ideal), and mold into a desired shape. Place another similar board over to create a 'sandwich' and proceed to clamp all four corners. Tighten each clamp a little at a time to squeeze out the water. Leave clamped for twenty-four hours.

5. Remove clamps and carefully lift the top board a few centimeters at a time, using a large spatula to prize away any strips of paper that may have stuck to the board. Use the spatula again, gently slide the blade under the re-cycled page and remove from the bottom board.

6. Place the damp page onto a wire mesh or a dry wooden board and place in a cool, dark and dry atmosphere. Turn the page every twelve hours until completely dry. Your re-cycled page is now ready to be displayed according to your taste.

# PREFACE

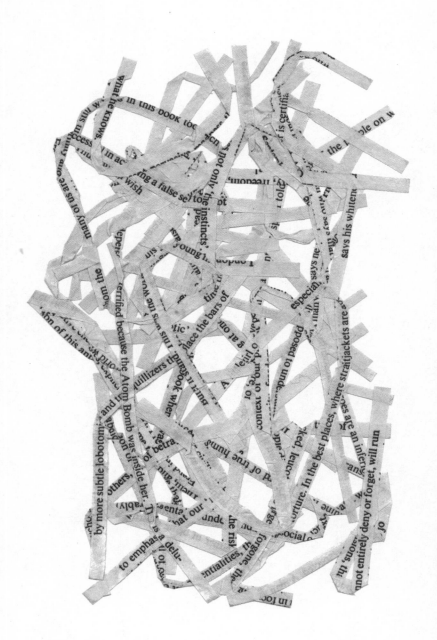

## The Gutenberg Fetish

Of course we cannot easily read the reified/vandalised text as such, and would need extremely highly developed memories to associate these fragments with something as specific as a stretch of text in the original book. We know about the heresy of the burning of the books (the 'heresy' of burning heretical books or the heresy of burning 'heretical' books). We know about the *trahison des clerks*, but the actual books themselves, as in book burnings, are a relatively minor development in the process. In book burning proper it is ideas and the people who produced them that are under attack. Some regard such attacks as heresy, as striking at the gods of the intellect. Here lies R. D. Laing et al; whatever truths were told us are merely pulp fiction now.

Chicago, where Stewart completed his MFA, is noted for its modern architecture and its economics - modern structures, modern markets. Perhaps what this intellectual fetishistic project reminds me of most is memorials or relics. The oblongs of pulped text are like squashed nests or

# ACKNOWLEDGEMENTS

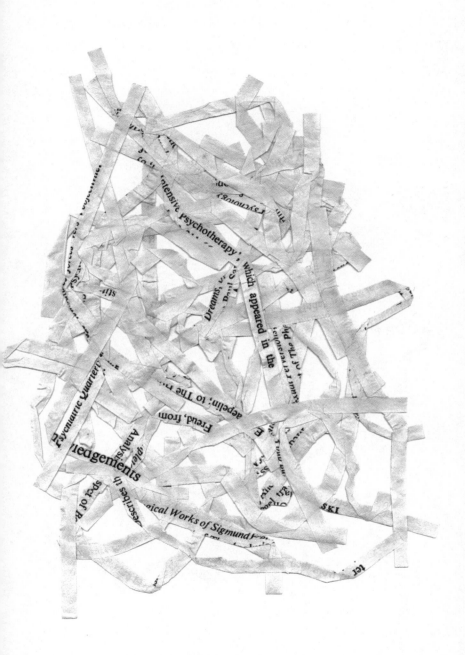

*George Szirtes...*

pelts - urgent but loose little shapes,
which have failed to become official
notices or part of the Dead Sea Scrolls.
Language is reduced to isolated words,
the pulp no longer holds the voice. One
could hardly call this an affirming gesture,
yet gesture is what it is: an urchin sticking
out its long red tongue at 'wisdom'.

Consider these two passages from the
Irish humourist Myles na Gopaleen, also
known as Flan O' Brien:

1) "You know the limited edition
ramp... Only 300 copies will be printed,
you say, and then the type will be broken
up for ever. Let the connoisseurs and
bibliophiles savage each other for the
honour and glory of snatching a copy...
Three hundred copies of which this is
Number 4,312. Hand-monkeyed
oklamon paper, indigo boards in
interpulped squirrel-toe, not to mention
twelve point Camile Perpetua cast
specially for the occasion. Complete,
unabridged, and positively unexpurgated.
Thirty-five bob a knock and a gory livid
bleeding bargain at the price.

"Well, I have decided to carry this

ACKNOWLEDGEMENTS
*(reverse)*

*13*

# PART ONE *Chapter I*

---

*The existential-phenomenological*
*foundations for a science of persons*

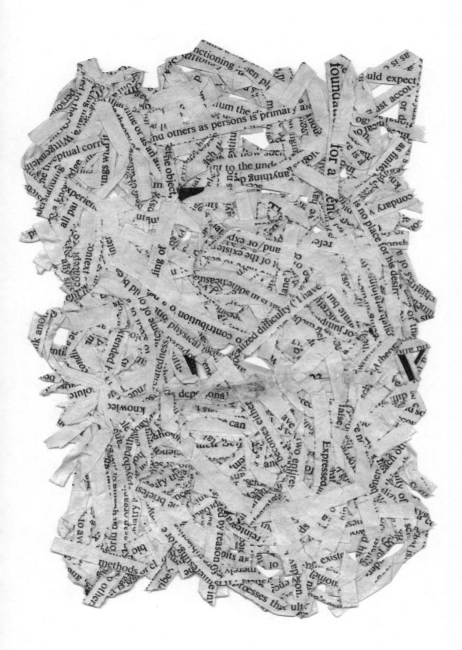

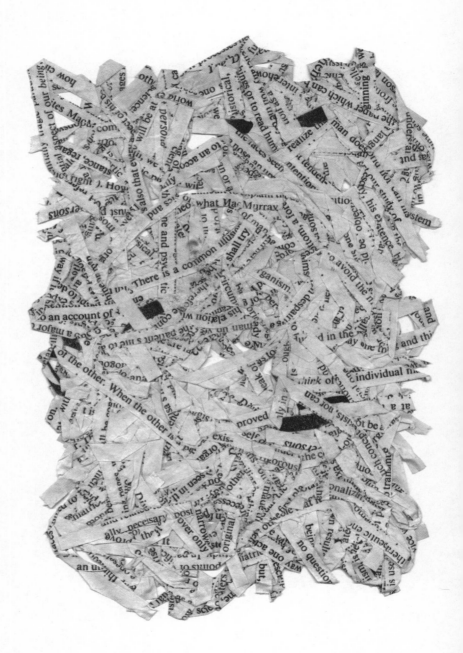

16

thing a bit farther... look out for the catch. When the type has been set up, it will instantly be destroyed and NO COPY WHATEVER WILL BE PRINTED...

"The charge will be five shillings. Please do not make an exhibition of yourself by asking me what you get for your money... you do yourself the honour of participating in one of the most far-reaching experiments ever carried out in my literary workshop."

2) "My friend is a man of great wealth and vulgarity. When he had set about buying bedsteads, tables, chairs and what-not, it occurred to him to buy also a library... This is what set me thinking. Why should a wealthy person like this be put to the trouble of reading at all? Why not a professional book-handler to go in and suitably maul his library for so much per shelf?... No machine can do the same work as the soft human fingers... Supposing an experienced handler is asked to quote for the handling of one shelf of four feet in length. He would quote thus under four heads:-

"Popular Handling - Each volume to

# PART ONE *Chapter II*

---

*The existential-phenomenological
foundations for the understanding of psychosis*

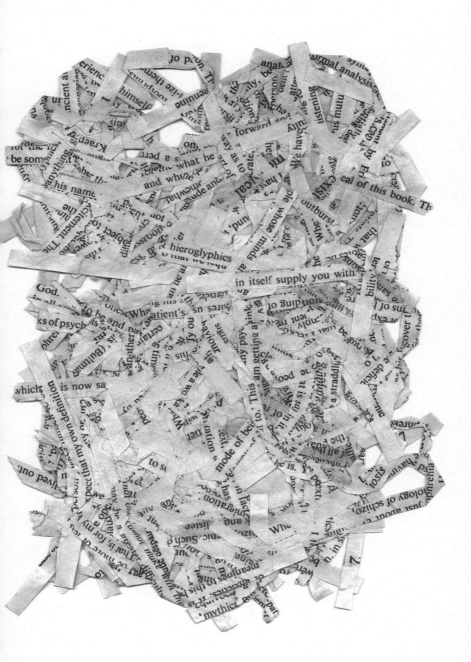

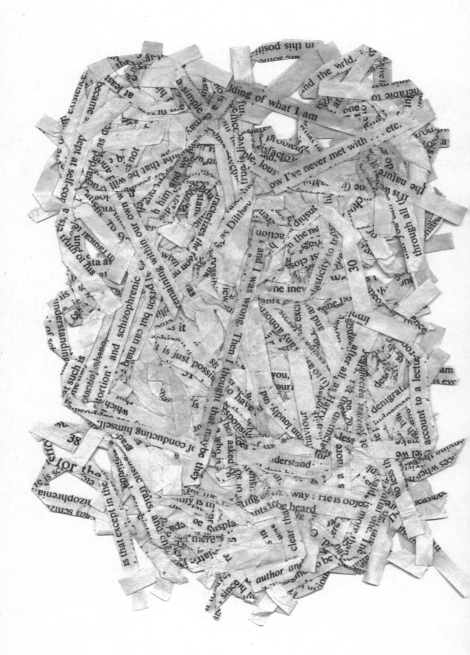

be well and truly handled, four leaves in each to be dog-eared, and a tram ticket, cloak room docket or other comparable article inserted in each as a forgotten bookmark, say £1 7s 6d. Five per cent discount for civil servants.

"Premier Handling - Each volume to be thoroughly handled, eight leaves in each to be dog-eared, a suitable passage in not less than 25 volumes to be underlined in red pencil, and a leaflet in French on the works of Victor Hugo to be inserted as a forgotten bookmark in each", etc, etc.

This supports the fetish theory, of course, but I have objections. All objects are potential fetishes. All acts are potentially erotic. But to talk of books as though they were predominantly, or even frequently fetishes is to employ cheap-thrill language to sex up a slender intellectual act. The sex is associational and in many ways restricted in its traditional habits. You can dress things in red and black, you can make them look rubbery or lacy, you can refer to sado-masochism or the features it is recognised

**PART ONE**
*Chapter II*
*(reverse)*

# PART ONE *Chapter III*

---

*Ontological insecurity*

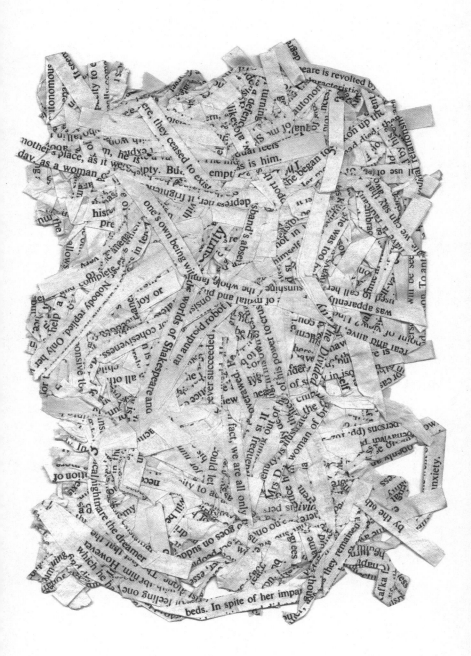

23

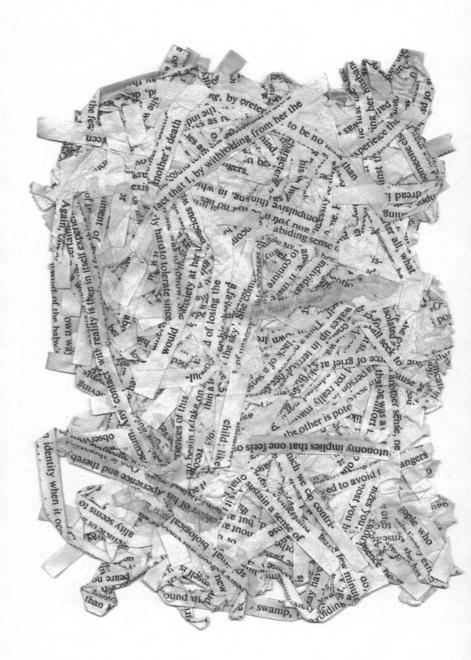

24

by, but reading a book, under normal circumstances, does not constitute an erotic experience. When you are reading - really reading - you forget the object altogether, until it grows heavy or you have to turn the page.

The breaking up of a text and its reorganisation into another book-like form, is the maximising of the potential intellectual tease of the fetish, that knows it is a fetish, and at the cost of minimising the reading experience. Certainly, it treats of reification and commodification. Something that began with one person modifying the thoughts and responses of another, as part of a long chain of such modifications and responses, is materially transformed into a gesture about the means. Gestures may be striking and even beautiful, but they don't cost. Or at least what they cost is not immediately apparent. The hidden cost is that the more the world is transformed into gesture the greater, and more comprehensive, the vacuum in which the gesture floats. Sawing off the branch you sit on is a form of tragedy. In

# PART TWO *Chapter IV*

---

*The embodied and unembodied self*

27

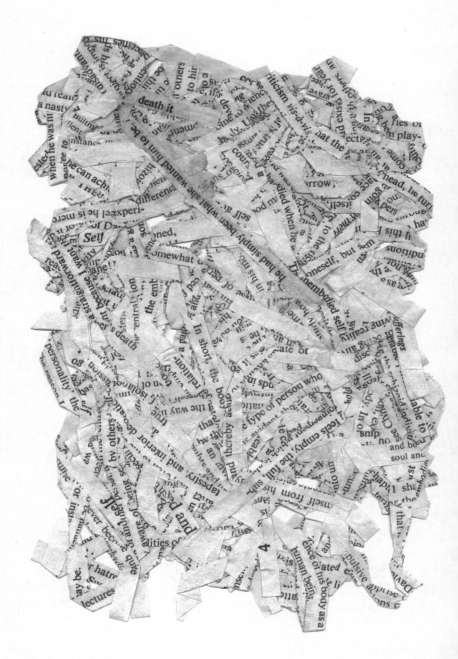

this sense tragedy is not dead. The world
is its own hero, diminishing into irony at
the far end of a reversed telescope. Art
may have become ever more like a reversed
telescope but life continues different.

I understand the pulped Laing, but it
chills me as gallery art often does now
and often means to. We seem to have
hollowed ourselves out, extracted the
marrow of history from our bones
and pulped it into an art of absolute
gestures. There is no breathless jangling
of bells to welcome the post-Gutenberg
galaxy. Perhaps there is nobody left to
jangle them. ■

**PART TWO**
*Chapter IV*
*(reverse)*

# PART TWO *Chapter V*

*The inner self in the schizoid condition*

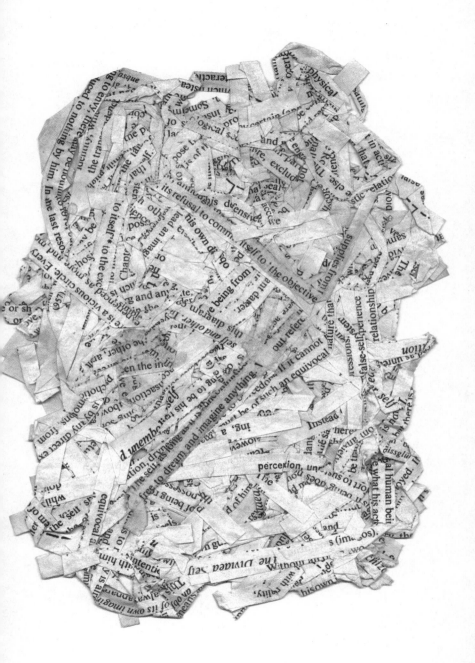

**Buzz Spector**

## Reading Material

A procedural injunction famously ascribed to Jasper Johns reads as follows: "Take an object. Do something to it. Do something else to it."[1] This notion, of starting with a thing and making it into art by subsequent alterations, can be traced back to Marcel Duchamp's readymades and altered found objects. This essay is concerned with the artistic altering of that particularly eminent object, the book. The art of Graham Stewart is my subject here, but an understanding of his work with the book as subject and object necessitates the inclusion of some historical predecessors.

We are well enough aware of the material attributes of books, although the current protocols of reading them and/or owning them suggest differing degrees of importance for these attributes. The body of the book - as distinct from the textual body of its words - is its sequence of pages, in various densities and heft; its signatures (suites of pages created by folding large sheets of paper, later trimmed) sewn together within the protective curve of the spine or cut in

**PART TWO**
*Chapter V*
*(reverse)*

# PART TWO *Chapter VI*

*The false-self system*

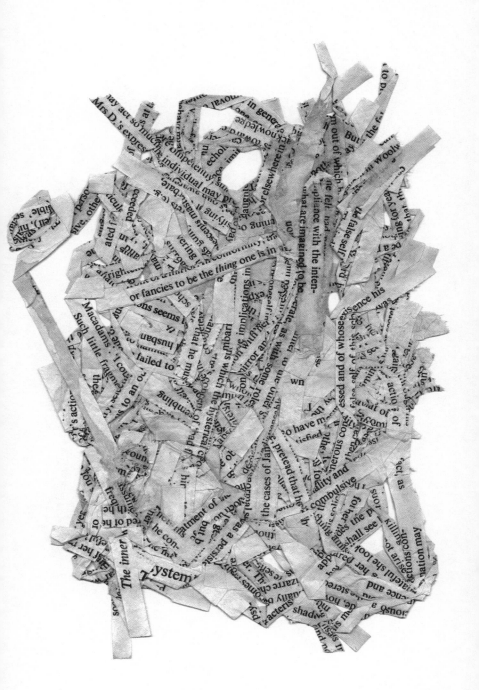

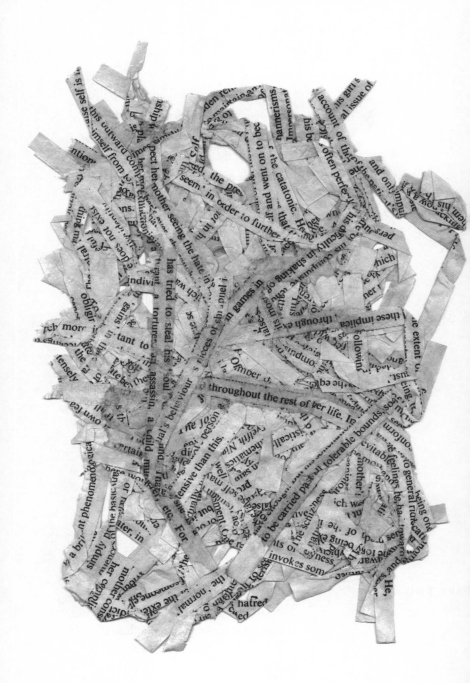

perfect alignment and bound together with glue; and its covers, in cloth over boards or of paper. In all these parts, as well as in the forms of the letters and methods of their placement upon the spread pages, the elements of a syntax is less connected to the narrative of the author than to such constructs as the "vocabulary" of a painter or the "syntax" of sculptor.

Notable among Johns' altered objects is his *Book* (1957), which uses a found hardcover volume as an armature upon which to paint with red encaustic. The book, mounted in the open position, remains recognisable, but the translucent medium that covers it obscures the typography of its two visible pages. Max Kozloff typifies Johns' artistic method as encouraging viewers to become readers, in effect, turning the process into narrative, and allows himself a moment of humour in describing *Book*: "If the pun is excusable, the work is all 'booked up' with thought."[2]

The quality of Kozloff's humour aside[3], his assertion of a pun into the

## PART TWO *Chapter VII*

*Self-consciousness*

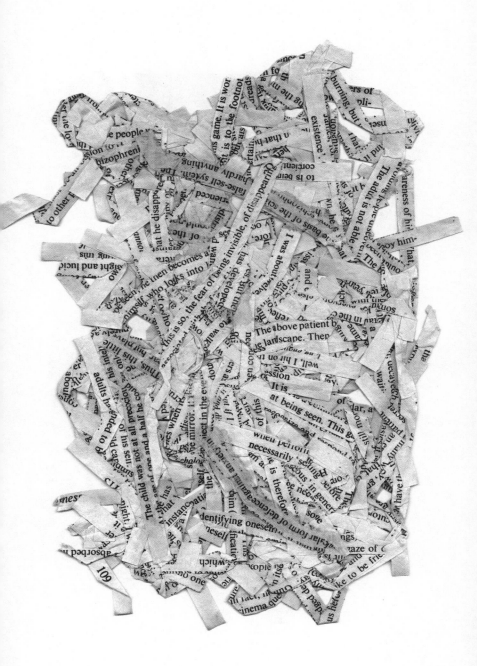

39

discourse on a book (-object) stands in intriguing proximity to the emotional supplement in the title of Duchamp's single use of a book in his art, *Unhappy Readymade* (1919). Duchamp sent this work in the form of a textbook of spatial geometry, to his sister, Suzanne, on the first occasion of her wedding to the painter Jean Crotti. Duchamp instructed Suzanne to suspend it from the ceiling of her balcony until it was destroyed by wind and rain. Duchamp offered a clue to his motivation in an interview with Pierre Cabanne:

"...the wind had to go through the book, choose its own problems, turn and tear out the pages... It amused me to bring the idea of happy and unhappy into readymades, and then the rain, the wind, the pages flying, it was an amusing idea..."[4]

Duchamp's rational has a certain apologetic aspect, recognisable in his reiteration of the amusement the gesture provided him. Later on the humour must have dissipated, for *Unhappy Readymade* is one of the few from his (lost) originals

**PART TWO**
*Chapter VII*
*(reverse)*

# PART TWO *Chapter VIII*

---

*The case of Peter*

43

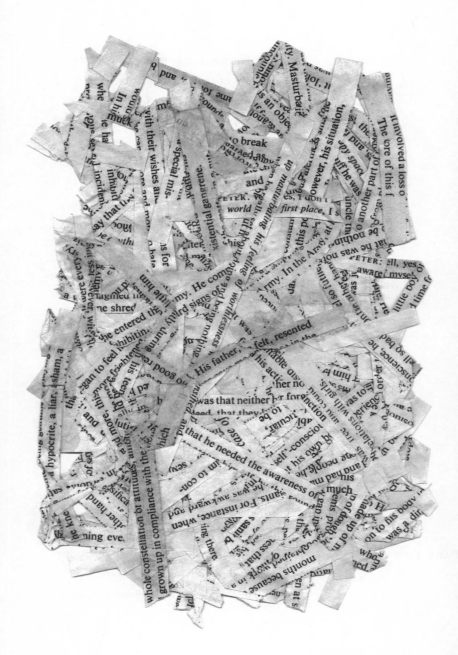

44

that Duchamp did not re-create for the editions of readymade multiples he published with Galeria Schwartz, Milan, in 1964.

John Latham didn't entrust the elements with the destruction of the book he chose to alter, Clement Greenberg's *Art and Culture,* in 1961. Latham borrowed the book from the St Martin's School of Art Library and together with friends and students, tore, chewed, and spat a number of its pages into a bowl. The distilled residue of this activity was returned to the library a year later, in a sealed test tube, in response to an inquiry about the overdue volume. Richard Hamilton notes that the method of Latham's experiment marks it as an important early example of "concept art," and informs us of the results: "Latham was sacked from his teaching job - but the work is now part of the collection of the Museum of Modern Art, NY."[5] Another pun activates Latham's gesture, the production of a literal "culture" from his transgressive mastication of Greenberg's book.

The shadow of transgression falls upon

# PART THREE *Chapter IX*

*Psychotic developments*

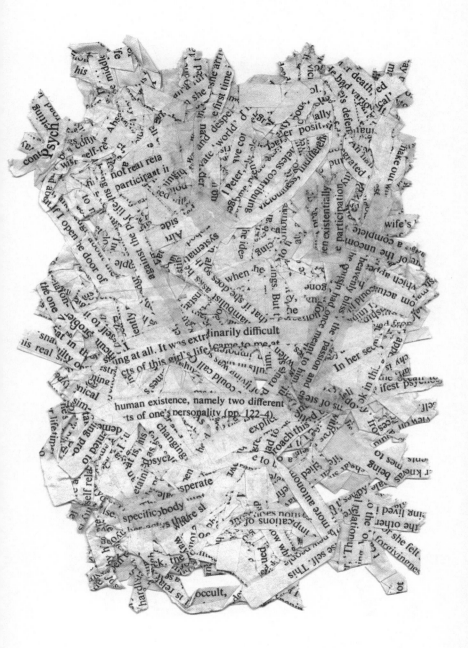

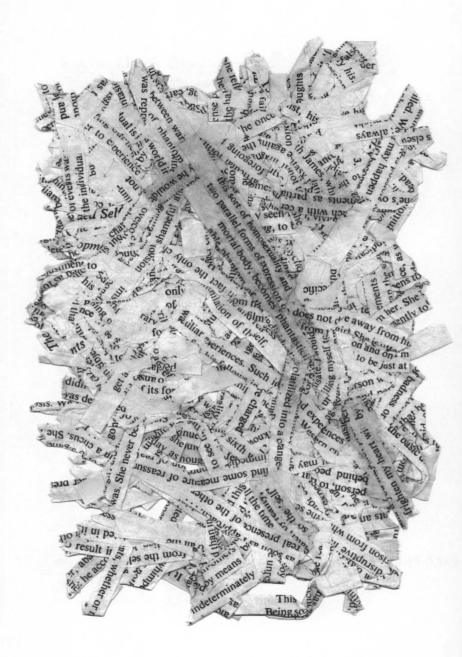

every altered book, for there is no
material alteration to be made upon a
given volume which does not draw our
attention away from its text and towards
a contemplation of that effect.[6] The
scope of the offense is a function of what
remains of the text. I do not speak of
legibility here as much as of identity; of
the author, the ideas, or the influence of
the book used in this way. In the case of
Johns, the altered book is framed so as to
make it completely unidentifiable.
Although some words are visible beneath
the application of translucent pigment,
Johns' painted object stands for all books,
and all that books stand for. Duchamp's
volume, unhappy with its dissolution, is
known to be a book of problems in
geometry. But which one? *Unhappy
Readymade* is different from Duchamp's
other chosen objects in that it had an
author. It is no accident, therefore, that
the "documentation" of this readymade
consists of a single fuzzy photograph and
a small oil painting, executed by Suzanne
Duchamp in response to Marcel's request
that she install it herself. From this record

**PART THREE**
*Chapter IX*
*(reverse)*

# PART THREE *Chapter X*

---

*The self and the false self
in a schizophrenic*

51

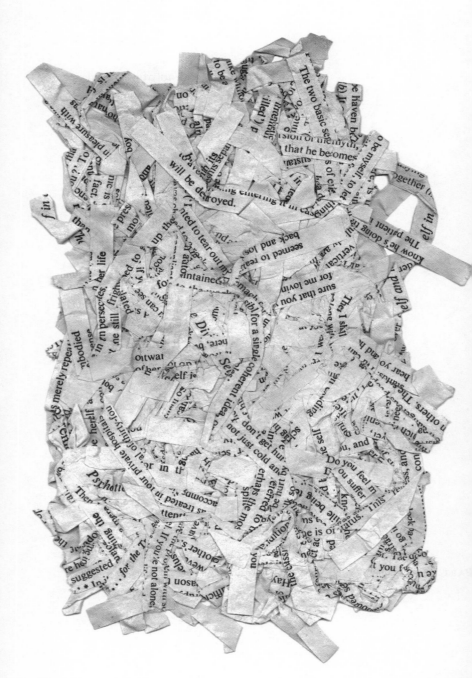

it is impossible to identify the particular edition chosen for the work. The book's employment as a generic exemplar was intended to overwhelm the specific text of the unknown geometrician contained within its covers, but it succeeds in that endeavour only through a lack of disclosure that operates quite differently from the given anonymity of whoever made the bicycle wheel, typewriter cover, or urinal. The effect of Latham's alteration of the Greenberg book is at least partially based on our awareness of both the celebrity of its author and the influence of his ideas about art: "[The] Modernist work of art must try, in principle, to avoid dependence upon any order of experience not given in the most essentially construed nature of its medium."[7] Latham's double meaning operates at the cognitive site where the organic residue of *Art and Culture* is understood to be the result of a rude (uncultured) process of chewing, spitting, and distilling its pages. Indeed, this trio of historical examples is more closely bound by a punning strain of humour

# PART THREE *Chapter XI*

---

*The ghost of the weed garden:*
*a study of a chronic schizophrenic*

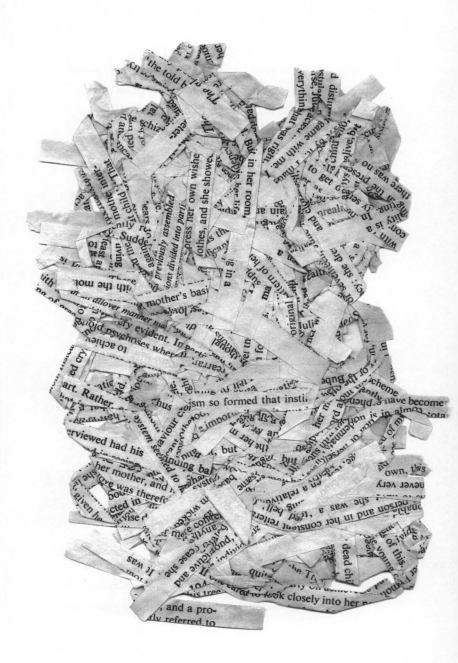

than by whatever text embeds it, provides
an accurate linguistic correlative to the
physical alteration of the book in its
function as armature for text.

There is an easily grasped pun in
Graham Stewart's book altering project,
*Shredded & Pulped.* The artist has taken a
copy[8] of R. D. Laing's influential and
controversial essay on the social context
of madness and run it through a paper
shredder, chapter by chapter, reducing it
to a pile of strips. That the book itself is
now divided is clear enough, but Stewart
isn't finished yet. He has collected the
strips of its eleven separate chapters, as
well as its acknowledgments, references,
and index, soaked them in water, mashed
them together into loaf-shaped blocks of
paper, and photographed them for
reproduction in the present volume. A
myriad of individual letterforms is visible
on the surface of each block, but any
meaningful words or phrases seen on
them can only be there by miraculous
coincidence. However, all the original
material of the copy with which Stewart
began is still present in this shredded and

# REFERENCES

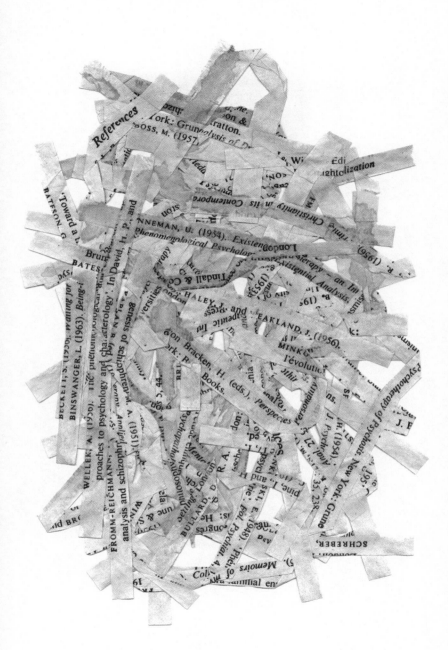

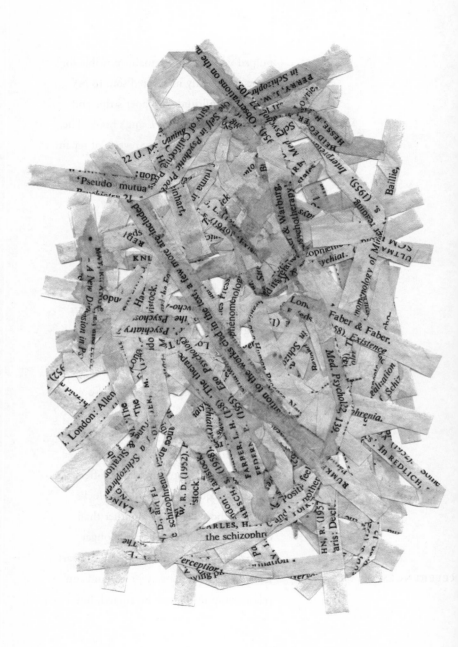

*Buzz Spector*

pulped version, so it remains possible for some sufficiently motivated soul to pry apart the multitude of paper strips and reconstruct the text of Laing's book. The recognition that this very reverie of repair and redemption parallels the healing drive of the doctor or therapist is another punning operation built into the work. Stewart's use of puns is key to understanding his selection of Laing's work for this project, for the pun is a rhetorical device capable of representing the bifurcate operations of the mind in Laing's model of a schizoid condition.

Crucial too, is the method of alteration to which Stewart has subjected *The Divided Self.* The artist "fed" the book through the mechanical jaws of a document shredder, a symbolic ingestion; he saved the residue of this action rather than letting it disappear, and he offers viewers a sequence of moulded blocks from the book he selected rather than displaying it as a formal, if no longer textual, unity. It would seem that Stewart has very little in the way of a "hands on" relationship to the text he altered, but

**REFERENCES**
*(reverse)*

# INDEX

Buzz Spector

this would be a misreading of how he
worked with his materials. The artist has
sorted through the shreds of the text,
gathered them according to the
structure of the pre-existing narrative,
and has formed them into blocks. If
destruction is apparent in this project,
so are its metaphors of harvesting,
grinding, kneading and baking. There is
figural bread here, a moral object the
equal of the book (or even more so since
bread possesses no subversive or
vituperative ingredients), and our
recognition of the tenderness in Stewart's
reconstitution of the *Divided Self* is
simultaneously appreciation of the way
the artist has given us an emblem of
sustenance and succour from his
imaginative transmogrification of its
paper into wheat, of its text into bread:
an artistic gesture becoming symbolic
food for thought. ■

*Buzz Spector*

1 I haven't seen these words in anything appearing under John's name, but there is a similar phrase, from the artists sketchbook, that states, "Take a canvas. Put a mark on it. Put another mark on it...(Ditto)." – Johns, Jasper. "Sketchbook Notes," Art and Literature, Spring 1965: p.192.

2 Kozloff, Max. Jasper Johns, New York: Harry N. Abrams, 1967: p.17.

3 There is, of course, another pun to be found in the relationship between the red that coats the pages of the book Johns found and its already having been read.

4 Cabanne, Pierre. Dialogues with Marcel Duchamp, New York: Viking Press, 1971: p.61. Cited in d'Harnoncourt, Anne, and McShine, Kynaston. Marcel Duchamp, New York: Museum of Modern Art, 1973: p.288-289.

5 Hamilton, Richard. John Latham: Early Works 1954-1972 (exh. Cat.) London: Lisson Gallery: p.8-9.

6 The symbolic moral and intellectual prestige of the book is always apparently sullied by its destruction, and such historical spectacles as the public burning of books attach the stigma of diabolical barbarism to the act.

7 Greenberg, Clement. "The New Sculpture," in Art and Culture, Boston: Beacon Press, 1961: p.139.

8 In point of fact, Stewart has altered more than one copy of Laing's book, for use in previous works of shredded and amalgamated text blocks. Indeed, the alteration and re-presentation of found texts is an ongoing aspect of Stewart's artistic practice, and since 1990 he has produced several extended series of altered books that focus on particular zones of culture (economics, law, philosophy, politics and psychoanalysis, among others), as well as making installations of different kinds of shredding machines in action upon selected texts.

genuine being – not his figure or shape, which would ex
'means' to convey by his ... or ... one might 'co
merely could do. In the same way, on the other hand,
... formance and his inner possibility, capacity, or intention
himself on the point and, after he has turned from b
the former *alone* is to be ...
in the act. Individuality, which commits itself to the obj
when it passes over into a deed no doubt puts itself to th

this – whether the deed is a real thing that holds togethe
and void and passes away. Objectification does not alter
it merely shows what the deed *is*, i.e. whether it *is* o
*nothing.*

It can readily be understood why the schizoid
... characterized by Hegel. The act is 's
minate, universal . . .'. But his self wishes to be con
*never* be what can be said of him. He must remain al
and the individual human being is ... such, and such
... never be what his act is. If he were what his
he would ... the mercy of any passe

simple fact that the act is, the individual is for others
what he seeks to avoid by the use of a false self so th
capacity, intention. The act is always the produc
... and the deed is never his true reality. He wi